Help!
I'm a
Junior High
Youth
Worker!

50 ways to survive and thrive
in ministry to early adolescents

P9-CEG-597

HELP!
I'M A
JUNIOR HIGH
YOUTH
WORKER!

50 ways to survive and thrive
in ministry to early adolescents

Mark Oestreicher

ZondervanPublishingHouse
Grand Rapids, Michigan
A Division of HarperCollinsPublishers

Help! I'm a Junior High Youth Worker!
50 ways to survive and thrive in ministry to early adolescents

© 1996 by Youth Specialties, Inc.

Youth Specialties Books, 1224 Greenfield Dr., El Cajon, CA 92021, are published by Zondervan Publishing House, 5300 Patterson Ave. S.E., Grand Rapids, MI 49530.

Library of Congress Cataloging-in-Publication Data

Oestreicher, Mark.
     Help! I'm a junior high youth worker! : 50 ways to survive and thrive in ministry to early adolescents / Mark Oestreicher.
        p.   cm.
     Includes index.
     ISBN 0-310-21328-2
     1. Church work with youth—United States. 2. Youth—United States—Religious life. I. Title.
BV4447.O47   1996
268'.433—dc21
                                   96-36848
                                     CIP

Edited by J. Cheri McLaughlin and Tim McLaughlin
Design by Patton Brothers Design

Printed in the United States of America

97 98 99 00/ /4

To the volunteer junior high workers I've worked with at Ward Presbyterian Church in Livonia, Michigan; First Baptist Church of Wheaton, Illinois; Christ Community Church in Omaha, Nebraska; Calvary Church of Santa Ana, California; and Lake Avenue Congregational Church in Pasadena, California.

CONTENTS

ACKNOWLEDGMENTS

Thanks to:
Curt Gibson (the guru of horror stories), Derrick Riggs,
Greg Lafferty, Eric Venable, Kara Eckmann and Jeff Meyers—
colleagues in ministry to junior highers and providers
of quotes, stories, and suggestions.
Jeannie and Liesl for allowing me the time to write.

JUNIOR HIGH WORKERS ARE THE COOLEST PEOPLE ON THE FACE OF THE EARTH. Or so I think. But working with young teens can be a head-spinning trip through a foreign land.

Have faith, O leader of impressionable people. Your work, whether it feels fulfilling (as it does at times) or worthless (as it also does at times), is a gift to God and a huge investment in the future.

God does amazing things through junior highers. They don't have to wait until they're high school students or adults to be used by God. He desires to radically work in and through their lives *now* to further his kingdom. Thank you for being part of that process.

This little book offers fresh perspectives, ideas, and encouragement about ministry to junior highers. It's about all those mundane yet profound details you face when you walk into the junior high youth room—what it means these days to be a junior higher, what sets them apart from older adolescents, what it means to *work* with junior highers, what they are and aren't capable of, how to connect with them in teaching or in just hanging with them.

If you lead a junior high group, chapter six is especially for you.

Sprinkled along the margins of *Help! I'm a Junior High Youth Worker!* are quotations from real junior high students and from experts in early adolescence. (Read more from these experts' works if you want a deeper study of early adolescence.) I've also thrown in some horror stories, just to remind you that you're not the only one who, in a miserable moment of middle school ministry, has wanted to disappear from the scene and never come back!

May God bless you in your ministry to junior highers!

FIRST THINGS FIRST
● ●

Axiom: Junior highers want to be treated like adults but still have the opportunity to act like children.

They're in-between. They're not kids anymore, but they sure act like it sometimes. They're certainly not adults yet, either—but they pretend to be. Accepting this dichotomy makes your work with junior highers much easier.

Axiom: Quality junior high ministry takes place in the context of meaningful relationships and meaningful ministry opportunities.

Your kids won't become spiritual giants because you deliver excellent youth talks. Your kids will grow spiritually when they see Christ at work in your life and then model themselves after you. They'll also grow spiritually when they do ministry. Focus your efforts on modeling Christ and steering kids into ministry.

Axiom: The single most important element of any meeting, event, or program is to know why you're doing it.

Purposeless junior high ministry is only negligibly different from baby-sitting. Without a purpose, nothing you can do has excellence.

My parents are like mosquitos: little by little they suck me dry.
—Nate, 13

So Just What Is a Junior Higher, Anyway?

Golden Rules

Keeping the atmosphere of your junior high meetings somewhere between a morgue and a piranha feeding frenzy is the constant challenge of young teen ministry. I've developed a handful of rules essential to conducting a successful junior high meeting.

▶ Don't mess with other people or their stuff.

▶ Don't talk when others are talking.

▶ No making fun of others or calling them names.

▶ Handouts are not to become airplanes, confetti, or doodle pads.

▶ Launching airborne objects, paper or otherwise, will result in death. (Feel free to soften the penalty here; but the rule's good).

For more on enforcing rules, see **Discipline Is a Happy Word** on page 23.

Hundred to One Ain't Good

To say small groups are important in junior high ministry is like saying snow

I love God. He's my most fav person and my best friend.
—*Sherie, 13*

is important to winter. (See **Small Is Good** on page 19.) Junior highers interact in small groups differently than high school students, however. Issues of discipline, self-image, and gender can send a discussion careening off the topic.

Trial and error taught me two good student-to-leader ratios for junior high small groups: 6:1 and 10:2. One adult leader can effectively lead a small group of about six young teens; a group that grows past six works better with two adult leaders. My *best* format for a junior high small group is about ten kids with two leaders. One leader teaches while the other one polices and supports. And they won't have to find substitutes, since one can cover for the other.

Finally, small groups with young teens *always* function more smoothly if they are made up of only one gender.

Won't You Pleeeeeease Work with Junior High?

Recruiting volunteer workers for junior high ministry turns up numerous skeptics—most of whom fall into one of the following three categories:

▶ People who hated their own junior high years and don't want to vicariously live them over again.

▶ People who falsely assume junior high-

I love lunch—it's a total calorie-fest!
—*Shellee, 13*

ers would never like them and who feel threatened when young teens don't accept them.

▶ People who falsely assume that only the young, crazy, musically gifted, stylish, funny, and media-savvy will succeed with young teens.

Help prospective volunteers to get past these three objections and you're home free (almost).

Sixth Sense

Many school districts have moved to a middle school model, grouping sixth through eighth grades together—thereby forcing churches to rethink the positioning of their sixth-graders.

Those not accustomed to imminent teens will undoubtedly perceive them as young and little (because they are). For years I resisted adding sixth grade to our junior high ministry. Yet I knew most churches tended to drop the ball with this crucial age group, boring them with childish curriculum and treating them younger than they are—despite the fact that many sixth-graders are taking their first steps into adolescence.

Now, after several years of working sixth-graders into the youth group, I love having them involved. At least three good options make effective ministry

Would You Stop Making That Splashing Sound During My Message?

The camp was in its third (of six) day when it hit the first kid. The camp nurse guessed it was the flu. Three more kids were in the infirmary by nightfall.

On the morning of the fourth day, the infirmary with a maximum capacity of four had a dozen young teens and counselors sprawled on cots. They entertained themselves by rating each other's vomit, weakly laughing through each trip to the toilet bowl.

By the evening of the fourth day, hurling hell broke loose. We couldn't make it through a meeting without junior highers and leaders losing it in the aisles. Cabin assignments became a joke as kids moved at will to those cabins with the least resident spew. Meals, as you might guess, were a complete waste of time.

The visiting doctor said it was "just a little virus." We cut the camp short.

Counselors and campers affectionately remember that week as Puke Camp.
—*Mark Oestreicher*

possible to these youngest of teens:

▶ You can lobby for a fifth and sixth grade preteen ministry. Run it like a youth ministry, as opposed to a children's Sunday school program, making it age appropriate and requiring high parental involvement.

▶ You can request that sixth-graders be incorporated into your junior high ministry—but still provide separate settings for most activities.

▶ If your sixth-graders are already combined with seventh- and eighth-graders, you can use grade-specific small groups to tackle sensitive subjects in age-appropriate ways.

No one in my school likes me, just because I'm short.
—*Kristina, 11*

SHOOTING AN ARROW

With their newly acquired abstract thinking ability (see **Cognitive Development** on page 25), junior highers can conceptualize what their futures might look like.

So suggest the future. As God gives you insight into the emerging strengths of different kids, shoot an arrow for them—help them see what the future might hold. You are in a powerful position to make an impression on junior high kids.

Case in point: my junior high youth pastor, whom I really looked up to, suggested that someday I'd be a youth pastor. He shot an arrow for me.

Af-Firm Suggestion

Your words carry power among your junior highers. You might question the truth of that statement when kids nod off right in the middle of your talk, leaving large drool stains down the fronts of their shirts. But it's true.

My school's okay. But it's all girls; so it's all gossip, all clothes, all pastel.
—*Monique, 13*

Here are four short syllables for you to remember whenever you use the power of your words: AF-FIR-MA-TION. They spell an important ministry—sometimes the most important. *Choose* to affirm kids. Do it all the time. Take care to affirm the annoying as well as the likeable kids.

Telling a plain girl she looks pretty today can change her world. Commenting to a short, uncoordinated boy that you really appreciate how he's always on time can carry him for days.

Affirm character. Affirm behavior. Affirm cool T-shirts. I don't care what you affirm—just find a way to do it. Affirming kids earns you the right to be heard, and that increases your effectiveness in ministry directly and indirectly.

Small Is Good

If your junior high group is small, don't sweat it. Our church culture has created an expectation that larger is always better. This is simply not true.

The advantages of a smaller group can be summed up in three words: intimacy, mobility, and flexibility. Small groups can really get to know each other and create a sense of family. I miss that when I'm working with a large group. With my small group, we could throw the whole gang in two cars and have Sunday school at the donut shop. We were ready to roll at any time—no planning necessary. And it was easy to be flexible. If we changed our plans at the last minute, it wasn't a big deal to call the parents.

Relish whatever size ministry God has given you—large or small.

THE WORLD'S WORST SELF-WORTH BAROMETER

The quickest route to your nearest state mental institution is to base your self-worth on relationships with junior highers or on what they say about you. Young teens add an entirely new dimension to the definition of *fickle*. If you cater to their every implicit and explicit suggestion of how you should reconstruct yourself, you'll be a different person each week.

In fact, allowing a junior higher to snub and spurn you once in a while builds your character. It's like a high-fiber muffin for the soul.

Family Knowledge

Junior highers are occasionally perplexing, to say the least. Just when you think you know a kid, she pulls something on you that sends you back to the drawing board.

Yet when you set the behavior of a young teen in the context of her *family*, the behavior often begins to make sense.

That's why you must get to know the families of the kids you minister to. Not only will you gain insight to increase your effectiveness in ministry, but you'll also receive solid support from parents. Opportunities to broaden your ministry can come your way, and some perplexing kids might begin to look like environmental products.

I was riding in the car, and I looked in the mirror, and all of a sudden it hit me: I look just like my mom!
—*Candace, 14*

I Was a Junior High Werewolf

One of the most enlightening ways to understand your junior highers is to reflect on your own young teen years.

WARNING: This can be very difficult. You should have a well of early adolescent memories, but it's not uncommon to bring up a dry bucket, empty of memories. Why? Sometimes because you had distasteful early adolescent experiences,

21

memories of which you may have blocked out. And sometimes junior high was simply a heck of a long time ago.

A few ideas to replenish your well of memories:

▶ Contact some old friends from your junior high years and reminisce.

▶ Walk the halls of your old junior high school. (Watch out—memories lurk around every corner.)

▶ Dig up your junior high yearbook and read the comments written by your friends.

School's like a vacuum—it sucks!
— *Nick, 14*

A friend of mine who has been involved in full-time junior high ministry for almost twenty years once told me, 'If you can learn how to run a junior high group, then you can rule the world.'
—*Wayne Rice,* Junior High Ministry *(Youth Specialties)*

THE B WORD

Balance. It sounds nice. So why is my pursuit of it usually an exercise in frustration? I tell myself balance is like holiness—no matter how hard I work at it, I won't get it right until I get to heaven. Still, I keep on working to be balanced (and holy). Like on a see-saw, when I come level for a split second, I seem to achieve balance only when I pass the midpoint of going from one imbalanced state to the next.

All this to say: don't let junior high ministry consume your life. As much as you may want to pour your life into young teens, maintain your spiritual and emotional sanity by drawing boundaries and setting limits.

- ▶ Decide your maximum amount of nights out per week and stick to it.
- ▶ If you're employed as a junior high worker, choose a day off and hold it in extra-high esteem.
- ▶ Spend time with friends your own age.
- ▶ Develop hobbies or interests that junior highers don't like.
- ▶ Don't look to junior highers to fill your friendship needs.
- ▶ Say no.

DISCIPLINE IS A HAPPY WORD

In most youth-work manuals "Junior High Ministry" is cross-referenced with "Discipline Issues." The two have been inseparable—and always will be. Yet it's time for a make-over of the image of discipline.

I only know my mom—not my dad. But I'll give you a clue about me and my mom—I live with my grandparents. Okay, I'll admit it. My mom beat me.
—*Angel, 13*

Discipline as case-by-case punishment for the purpose of maintaining a modicum of control is reactive and negative. Moving from reactive to proactive, however, casts discipline as positive.

To discipline proactively, set some good, logical rules (for suggestions see **Golden Rules** on page 15). Then communicate them like crazy, along with the consequences for noncompliance. Choose realistic and enforceable consequences.

Now for the art of discipline—that funny little balance that only *you* can find. The paradox inherent to discipline requires you to be flexible, yet without backing down.

Say you've set your expectations and communicated them. Everyone knows that they don't throw paper in the youth room. Then for no apparent reason, Christy wads up her handout (the absolutely brilliant one you spent hours creating last night) and chucks it down the row at David. No question—Christy faces the guillotine of your discipline. You've already laid down the consequences of actions like Christy's, and she knows them, too.

But now say that in a moment of sheer exuberance, when the whole youth group is standing on their chairs cheering you for the high quality of your latest talk, Christy innocently, in celebration, tosses her paper in the air. Obviously, you cut her some slack.

On my first Sunday at a new job, I taught to the sound of paper airplanes and wadded-up handouts swishing around the room. Right off I communicated a clear and strong rule: If you throw paper, you'll be asked to leave the room and sit in the hall. A few kids tested the rule and found it to be sure. Airborne paper wasn't a problem after that.

Sounds simple, doesn't it? It's not.

I love my parents more than anything in the world. My dad isn't a Christian, but I still love him so much. I really appreciate my parents and look up to them.
—*Melissa, 13*

DEVELOPMENTALLY SPEAKING

● ●

COGNITIVE DEVELOPMENT

This is the "biggie" of developmental changes during the early years of adolescence.

Kids are handed a perk when they enter the bittersweet glories of puberty: abstract thinking, for the first time in their lives. This cognitive change—that is, a change in how kids think—affects almost every area of growth and development. Imagine, for instance, how acquiring abstract thinking skills affects their concept of God. As children, they thought of God only in concrete terms. Now, with a larger collection of intellectual tools that includes abstract-thinking abilities, junior highers have whole new ways of viewing God, grace, salvation, relationships, power, motives, and just about everything else. It's revolutionary.

Like an untrained muscle, however, the new perceptions of early adolescents are on the flabby side. Effective junior high workers help kids exercise this "muscle" by challenging their childish faith and praising them for questioning. Give kids

Our relationship with our [13-year-old] son currently involves a certain amount of conflict, in the same sense that the Pacific Ocean involves a certain amount of water.
—*Dave Barry*, Dave Barry Is Not Making This Up *(Crown Publishers)*

room to doubt—and encourage anxious parents to value the process of doubting.

On the other hand, don't assume that *all* your junior highers can already think abstractly. The older or more mature ones probably can, but the younger ones may not be able to yet.

I truly believe that the most cost-effective program in any church is a strong junior high department. So our best efforts and budgeting need to be aimed at doing a good job with kids in this age bracket.
— *Doug Murren,* The Baby Boomerang *(Regal)*

LOVE ROLLER COASTER

As junior highers begin to think abstractly, they experience new emotions (and old emotions in new ways). This throws them into the most topsy-turvy, hot-and-cold time of their lives.

One minute Amy says, "I hate everyone!" A minute later she's gushing, "Jenny is the best friend anyone could ever have in the whole world!" Love and hate have new depths. Empathy is truly possible.

A young teen's experience of a romantic breakup, for example, is as real as an adult's more mature response to similar pain. Although adults downplay the teen's emotional trauma by saying, "You don't really know what love is yet," that junior higher's emotion at that moment is deeper than any they've ever known.

God made junior highers this way—and everything God makes is good. So enjoy their roller coaster vicariously. This emotional field-tripping can be fun! Just make sure your seat belt is strapped securely across your lap.

Social Butterflies

A child's social world is fairly simple. Friends live in the neighborhood, usually within a block or two. Maybe a friend from church lives across town.

Entering junior high, however, opens the door on a whole new world of social possibilities. Girls tend to form friendship groups of two or three. Most female friendship groups of four eventually split in half.

Junior high boys, on the other hand, run in packs. The makeup of the male pack of friends can change constantly, just as the inner circle of girls' friendships can change.

The social scene also impacts self-image. Whereas a preteen's self-image is usually self-defined and defined by parents, junior highers form their self-image based heavily on peer input.

Friendships with the opposite gender begin taking on entirely new dimensions. Yet few male-female friendships make it through puberty without dissipating, especially because girls tend to mature so much earlier than boys.

He's a Big God

The spiritual development of young teens ties in directly with cognitive development

Anatomical Awareness

In a special drawer I keep a few old clothes just to wear on mission trips. Once among these work clothes was a favorite pair of jeans that had a few small holes in the seat, none of which were especially noticeable. The biggest hole was only about an inch, and it revealed only the harmless pattern on my boxer shorts.

While working with a half dozen junior highers on the roof of a building project, I did a lot of bending over as I taught and retaught the correct method of nailing shingles. After a couple hours of this, I started hearing small rips each time I bent over. I reached behind me and felt a now rather substantial hole in my jeans.

No more bending over, I thought. I can teach kids how to roof standing up. Too soon, however, I forgot myself, bent over again, and ripped some more. I stood up straight and, thinking only of my jeans and not of my anatomy, commented to my junior high roofing team, "Gosh, my butt hole just keeps getting bigger and bigger."
—*Mark Oestreicher*

(see **Cognitive Development** on page 25). Because they gain the ability to think abstractly, *everything* about Christianity takes on fresh nuances and meanings. Think of it this way: young teens have acquired new word-processing software, so to speak, and they're trying to convert their last ten years' worth of accumulated files into a new format.

Young teens are reformatting their files about God, salvation, grace, the Incarnation, and almost every other spiritual topic. They're also reformatting the input from their parents' faith in order to form their own spiritual identities.

My contention, completely unproven by legitimate study, is that young teens *must* reenlist in the faith in the same way a soldier recommits to the army. If young teens don't internalize their faith, making it their own, their faith will stagnate by their middle teen years.

Help parents enjoy their teen's doubts and questions. When a parent reports with anguish that their kid has just said, "I'm not sure I want to be a Christian anymore," I always respond by saying, "That's excellent!" After I explain why, their look of shock melts into relief.

Help kids question their faith. Force them to think in new ways. Enjoy this process.

Adolescence is believed to start earlier because puberty starts earlier. Today, some females begin menstruating as early as eleven—150 years ago it wasn't until 16. Boys usually kick in at around 13. We are not sure why the age continues to drop.
—*Chap Clark, chairman of Denver Seminary's youth ministry department, in an* Ivy Jungle Report *interview, Spring 1996*

Between a Rock...

I would be foolish enough to attempt to describe junior highers in just two words only if I were on the rack—in which stretching circumstances I'd choose the words *in-between* and *change*.

Junior highers are not *there* yet, but neither are they where they were. They're not children—but they're not adults, either. Even the moniker JUNIOR HIGH says "not yet high school." I've had boys who talk about sex one minute and cartoons the next. I've met girls wearing fashion nails and perfect make-up who still play with Barbie dolls. Young teens are in-between.

Junior highers live in-between because so much about them is changing. They go through more physical, emotional, social, mental, and spiritual changes than they will at any other time of their lives. Only infants experience more physical change. Little boys and girls turn into young men and women right before our eyes. Obviously, the junior high years are a critical time in the developmental cycle.

Now give me a hand down off this rack.

Line Trouble

Observe a fifth-grader with her parents. For the most part they still have open and clear communication. She is able to

Early adolescence is a uniquely critical time in human development. During this frequently overlooked period of growth and change, young people emerge from the dependence of childhood to face the freedom, responsibility, and conflicting values of adulthood.
—*Early-adolescence authority Joan Scheff Lipsitz, quoted in* Understanding Early Adolescence: A Framework, *by John P. Hill (Center for Early Adolescence)*

29

embarrass her parents with her innocently candid questions. And if the family doesn't suffer serious dysfunction, she enjoys spending time with her parents.

Now look at the same girl as a tenth-grader. Her communication with her parents is limited to a few short sentences on the two nights a week the family actually eats dinner together, and she asks her parents questions only when it's absolutely necessary. Spending time with her parents socially is punishment to her.

This extreme example is sadly common. What happened?

Family therapist Mary Pipher writes in *Reviving Ophelia* that within American families, the distancing of family members from each other almost always begins in junior high and creates a great deal of tension in families. She observes that

> parents set limits to keep their daughters safe, while daughters talk about rights and resent what they see as their parents' efforts to keep them young. Parents are fearful and angry when their daughters take enormous risks to prove they are independent.

Since lines of communication between parents and teens commonly deteriorate in junior high, we need to orchestrate communication between parents and teens. (See **Family Fitness** on page 56). Talk with kids about their relationships with

Something dramatic happens to girls in early adolescence...the selves of girls go down in droves. They crash and burn in a social and developmental Bermuda Triangle. They lose their resiliency and optimism and become less curious and inclined to take risks...more deferential, self-critical and depressed.
—*Mary Pipher,* Reviving Ophelia: Saving the Selves of Adolescent Girls *(Ballantine)*

their parents. Expose them to examples of clear family communication, and help them to see the benefits of it.

I Gotta Be Me!

Time for a big word: *individuation*. Individuation is the process that teens— and young people even into their twenties—go through to answer the question, Who am I?

It's a super-important process that starts with the onset of puberty.

Most high schoolers are well into this process. When you look at a 17-year-old, you can often tell what he'll be like when he's 30.

Junior highers, on the other hand, offer few clues to the kinds of people they'll be. They have no idea themselves— but they desperately want to find out. That's why young teens try so many things.

James is a three-sport boy, not to mention his afternoons in Science Club and Computer Club. He visits Virtual World two times a week for virtual-reality gaming, and he's active in his church junior high group. Crystal sings in her school *and* church choirs, toots the trumpet in band and orchestra, plays volleyball and softball, participates in Foreign Language Club, and attends Young Life on Tuesday

"The thing that causes the most stress in my life, more than anything else, is choosing what I'm going to wear to school tomorrow. I stand in front of my closet for a half hour or an hour every night wondering if I'll get made fun of." *Brad, 13*

nights.

Young teens try tons of things to find the ones they're good at. It's all part of individuation—of defining one's self.

ARMPIT HAIR AND ZITS

The physical changes triggered at puberty are enough to wreck anyone's life, at least temporarily. Along with trying to manage voices that warble indecisively over the span of an octave or two, boys often (though not always) experience a major growth spurt. Chests broaden, muscles become more defined. They sprout hair on legs, arms, under armpits, and in the pubic area. They start to sweat (and stink). Hormones race through their bodies like kids at a water park. And as if all this isn't enough, they get erections and have wet dreams. It really is a Jekyll and Hyde thing.

I remember when I first noticed dark hair on my legs. It appeared mid-calf and below—on the part of my leg, I noticed, that was covered by my groovy striped sweat socks. Using my new cognitive abilities, I reasoned that hair grew best in the dark, where socks or pants covered the skin. So for an entire summer I baked in long pants instead of shorts, in a heroic effort to get my leg hair to grow.

Then there are the female changelings.

My mom and dad used to fight a lot, but they are working out their problems with a counselor. This helps me to get along with them a lot better. My dad is a youth pastor.
—Becka, 13

They typically hit puberty about two years earlier than boys (that's a little before eleven years old). Girls change even more than boys. The entire shape of their bodies shift. Breasts develop and hips widen. Hair shows up in all the same places it does for boys, as does sweat and body odor—and menarche. (I remember period jokes circulating during my own junior high years. Now that I think back on them, it's clear that neither I *nor* the boys who told me the jokes understood the first thing about menstruation.)

Here are a few tips for those who minister with kids living in the in-between:

Our church is good except that it now starts at 9:15. My family couldn't make it on time when it started at 9:30.
—*Joshua, 12*

▶ If a boy adamantly refuses to stand up, don't make him. Spontaneous erections can cause extreme embarrassment (even if no one else knows).

▶ Always enlist both male and female leaders for trips. Not only is this better for ministry purposes, it will protect you from getting stuck in an awkward situation.

A friend of mine led a canoe trip with a mixed group of teens, but only male leaders. During the trip a girl was stung by a bee on her nipple. Although the girl insisted that my friend remove the stinger, he refused. He's still employed and not in jail.

▶ If you take girls on a trip where you

Got the Munchies?

It was my first Sunday as the junior high assistant at a very large church, and my boss, the junior high pastor, was making me teach.

When I get nervous, I say things off the cuff that I later regret.

I don't have a clue now what I was speaking about. But somehow I decided that the movie I'd watched on TV the night before illustrated my topic. *Alive*, you may remember, was about the plane that crashed in the Andes. The passengers weren't found for months, and those who survived did so by resorting to cannibalism. I can't now recall the connection of this movie to my talk, but at the time I thought it was brilliant.

I asked the students if they'd seen the movie. A few had. Then I asked, "Did you see what part of the dead people they ate first?"

I could see my new boss's eyebrows rise.

In the movie, the uncertain survivors had sampled the back upper thighs of their unlucky fellow passengers. With exaggerated humor and larger-than-life body motions, I plunged ahead and proclaimed, "I mean, I like butts, but I don't like to eat them."

It's a miracle I kept my job.
—*Derrick Riggs, Ward Presbyterian Church, Livonia, Mich.*

won't be near stores, ask a female leader to bring along feminine pads and tampons in case a girl starts her period and isn't prepared.

▶ Never, never make fun of kids' changes. Mimicking a boy's breaking voice, or teasing a girl—even good naturedly—about her new femininity, can crush a kid.

▶ Set ground rules to keep the hormones in check—especially on trips.

▶ Realize that premature development—whether height, breast growth, or any other change—almost always makes kids self-conscious.

▶ Allow kids privacy when they change clothes on trips. Don't tease them for not dressing in front of others.

TIME TO TEACH

SAY WHAT?

Junior highers are ten times more likely to remember what *they* say than what *you* say. They even remember what they think more than what you say. That's why those who can get kids to share their opinions are practically royalty.

Use creative questioning regularly in your teaching. Plan questions that lead you and your students down a path of discovery. Don't be afraid to throw in some questions off the top of your head, either—even some silly ones.

And remember that while content questions have their place, the best questions don't have one right answer.

Most people feel totally unequipped to work with [junior highers]. All it really takes, however, is someone who will love them in the midst of all their diversity, and someone who will look at the big picture and wait for God to bear fruit in His time, not theirs.
—*Greg Johnson, quoted in Reaching Kids before High School by Dave Veerman (Victor)*

PENCILS UP

So, you've faced the bitter truth that junior highers don't remember much of what you, their profound and eloquent teacher, say.

So get kids writing. Asking them to record their own opinions on paper before they share answers keeps their answers distinct and un-peer-polluted.

Other ways to get kids writing—

▶ Set up your topic by having kids answer a survey.

▶ Pass out a list of content questions to guide your students through a Bible passage.

▶ Ask them to record (in a journal) changes they need to make.

▶ Give them their choice of crazy postcards to write thank-you letters to their parents.

HOOK, BOOK, LOOK, TOOK

Youth ministry pioneer Larry Richards developed a catchy outline for your teaching time. As you prepare your lesson, thinking through the four components—hook, book, look, took—ensures that you get where you want to go.

Hook *Why do I care about this subject?*
Book *What does the Bible say?*
Look *What does the Bible mean?*
Took *How do I apply this?*

THAT WAS LEARNING?

Junior high ministry should be fun. And no, fun is not merely a secular goal. If Jesus had taught junior high, I think he would have had a riot. Make your teaching fun with learning games. Games also

36

help lower students' defenses as they interact with each other. Try some of these ideas:

▶ **King of the Mountain.** Use this variation to introduce a session about peer pressure: ask half the group to hold a pose while the other half of the group tries to knock them off balance.

▶ **Charades.** Form teams that act out specific emotions. Then discuss the part emotions play in relationships.

▶ **Popular Music Mystery.** Form two teams. Assign each team to think of three popular, current love songs. Team One hums the first line of the song while Team Two guesses the title and the performing group. Have the whole group sing the first line of the song. Then switch and let Team Two hum a mystery tune. Use the lyrics to lead into your discussion of love.

▶ **Win, Lose, or Draw.** This is Pictionary— but with words that relate to your topic. Form teams that attempt to communicate these words by illustrating them on a whiteboard, chalkboard, butcher paper, etc.

In other words, fun and learning are not mutually exclusive.

Distinct markers that once defined childhood are rapidly fading. Children who should be playing on swings are forced to deal with adult issues.
—*Doug Fields,* Too Old, Too Soon *(Harvest House)*

As vital as it is to minister to early adolescents, it is just as important to do it *right*. This means thinking through and designing your purpose, philosophy, and plan.
—*Dave Veerman,* Reaching Kids before High School *(Victor)*

TOP TEN TOPICS

Here they are for your dissection—my personal (and very subjective) list of the top-ten most important teaching topics for junior high ministry (in no particular order):

▶ **God's grace.** Kids must re-understand this during their young teen years (see **He's a Big God** on page 27).

▶ **Changes.** Help them get a clue about what's happening to them.

▶ **Sexuality.** Not just sex. Most junior highers, I've found, possess more misinformation than truth about their own sexuality. That they were created as sexual beings is a profound truth to junior highers.

▶ **Living for God.** Junior highers are capable of a deeper and more meaningful walk with Christ than most adults allow them to attain.

▶ **Why believe?** What's the point of being a Christian? Every kid asks this question at some time during the teen years. Address it head-on.

▶ **Making good decisions.** More than anything else, kids want to make their own decisions. So the best long-range work you can do with junior highers is helping instill in them the habit of evaluating choices before they make them, and then making wise decisions from among the options.

- ▶ **Friendships.** How do they work? How do I start them? How do I keep them? What about cliques? What about fights?
- ▶ **Family.** It's a war-zone out there for two-thirds of your kids; and a semi-blissful naive home life for the other third.
- ▶ **Basics of the Faith.** Why church? What's the deal with worship? Why should I pray? How do I pray? Is the Bible reliable?
- ▶ **Who are God and Jesus?** Separate myths and childish misconceptions from the truth.

> Fear of rejection can become a source of anxiety and stress, often dictating behavior patterns and value choices. Middle schoolers will usually do whatever is most conducive to making friends and keeping them. Having friends is, quite simply, the lifeblood of adolescence.
> —*Wayne Rice,* Enjoy Your Middle Schooler *(Zondervan)*

WOULD YOU LIKE A ROLE WITH THAT?

Using role plays is a simple matter of assigning parts to a few kids, setting up a scenario, and watching them wing it: "Bobby, you're the dad. Jenna, you're the mom. Tina, you're their junior high daughter. Tina, you want permission to go to an all-night party at a friend's house. Go."

Youth work experts have been telling us for years how effective role-playing is in freeing kids to air their perspectives. Even the students in the audience pay closer attention when you've got a live case study to discuss.

On the other hand, in large groups most junior highers are too self-conscious to play their parts to any worthwhile conclusion. It's in small groups, where there's already a high-level of trust, that I use role-plays all the time. After a role-play, students eagerly discuss the topics presented.

TRY IT ON FOR SIZE

Most educational programs—including youth ministry—dispense knowledge, but do nothing to help translate knowledge to action. Simulations are one way of helping students bridge the gap between knowing and doing. Simulations create situations where young teens can, knowingly or unknowingly, "try on" new behaviors.

You don't need a graduate degree in education to create good simulations. Just ask yourself, "How can I set up a climate where my students can analyze choices and consequences without committing themselves?"

▶ Hand out play money to practice making choices about spending.

▶ After they fail at an impossible task, remove the penalty and talk about grace.

▶ Role-play what it would look like to be nice to your siblings when they're being jerks to you.

▶ Put kids in two groups. Set up a visit between two make-believe cultures—

In many respects moving from the culture of childhood to the culture of adolescence is like moving from one society to another; and the change in behavior and conduct the adolescent encounters can lead to a form of shock—peer shock.
—*David Elkind,* All Grown Up and No Place to Go *(Addison-Wesley)*

School is okay. It would be better if classes didn't get in the way.
—*Deborah, 12*

complete with different ways of greeting, conversing, and relating. After kids interact for a short time, invite them to talk about culture, racism, or missions.

CLIPPING

Although using self-produced video in your teaching is effective, shooting and editing your own videos may not be the best use of your resources. Only techno-wizards or people with way too much time on their hands can pull it off.

You can still throw in an occasional visual element to your teaching, though, and get in on one of the positive results of the industrial revolution. Here are two ways to do it:

▶ Use clips of TV shows, commercials, and rented movies to kick off a discussion or drive home a point. For example, show Indiana Jones taking his step of faith in the final minutes of *Indiana Jones and the Last Crusade*...choose a two-minute scene from *Clueless* to talk about materialism, money, values, or family relationships...watch Tom Hanks realizing he's lost in space in *Apollo 13*, and talk about feeling helpless.

▶ Although they're pricier than taping "Baywatch" on your home VCR, prepackaged youth ministry videos

What a Surprise! It's the Pastor's Kid!

I traveled with a bunch of junior high kids on a mission trip to a Native American Indian reservation in Arizona. The missionary pastor of the reservation church had a 13-year-old daughter who joined our group for the trip.

On the way we stopped by Wal-Mart to pick up supplies. The kids quickly dispersed throughout the store.

Not ten minutes passed before the manager paged me over the store intercom. As I approached the manager's office, I heard loud swearing. The missionary pastor's daughter had been caught shoplifting, and the girl felt the manager's threat to call the police gave her license to curse the manager like a sailor.

Ten minutes later I was driving our church van behind a police car containing one still-raving junior high-aged missionary pastor's daughter. Two-and-a-half hours later, the sheriff at the jail released her into my custody. What a thrill. I was tempted to let the sheriff keep her.
—*Curt Gibson, Pasadena First Church of the Nazarene*

are usually worth the investment. My suggestions: The entire *Edge TV* series (Edge Communications, 800/279-9210) and anything by Curt Cloninger—*God Views*, *Witnesses*, *Red-Letter Edition* (Gospel Films, 800/253-0413).

Listen Up!

The Video Age is here, but film is not the answer to all your junior high ministry yearnings. Every now and then try letting a dinosaur out of its cage—use audio resources. I know audio is limited, but no creative teaching tool can be used more than once in a while anyway. And audio stuff works, once in a while.

▶ Record a series of five- to ten-second song snippets related to your topic. Ask the kids to guess the topic by listening to the tape.

▶ Make an overhead with the lyrics of a relevant song. Play the song on your boom box while the kids read along.

▶ Add a few sound effects to your storytelling. Sound effects CDs are available at every music store.

Tell Me a Story

Young teens love stories—and the Bible is loaded with awesome stories. The problem is, most Bible translations aren't written to keep 12-year-olds on the edge of their seats.

If you think the solution is to tell the story in junior high language, you're only partly right. It's best not to totally ad-lib the story, or students can pick up the idea that the Bible doesn't contain anything worth reading. Instead find the delicate balance between word-for-word reading and embellishment of the narrative.

After familiarizing yourself with the story, select certain verses to actually read, and tell the rest of the story in the context of a young teen's world. This kind of Bible story telling takes a little practice, but it's worth it when you see your students eager to hear Bible stories—even if they've heard them since preschool.

> School is weird, because everybody tells you you'll appreciate it later. But you hate it so much, you don't know. But then I've never met anyone who regretted going to school.
> —*Dave, 13*

Take It On Home

Junior highers are pack-rats—they'll keep anything you give them until they're about 16. Okay, maybe not dinosaur stickers. But an occasional, carefully selected take-home item can be extremely cool. It can remind your students of the teach-

continued on page 46

My Top Ten

Here are my favorite resources for junior high ministry. Of course, by the time you read this there will be several new junior high resources on the market, and some may be excellent. Surf the shelves at your Christian bookstore. Call publishers of youth curricula and ask for their catalogs—Youth Specialties, Group Publishing, David C. Cook, Gospel Light, your denominational publisher, and the like.

The titles are in alphabetical order.

▶ *Creative Junior High Programs from A to Z: Vol. 1 (A-M)*, Steve Dickie and Darrell Pearson (Youth Specialties, 800/776-8008). I thought this was a geeky idea when I first heard about it. But I'm using it right now for my Sunday morning lessons...and I love it. The lessons are active and fun, with lots of variety.

▶ *Custom Curriculum* (David C. Cook, 800/426-6596). There are sixteen titles in the young teen line (and another sixteen in the high school line). They are extremely well-written and packed with creative ideas. The real joy of this curriculum is the sheer quantity of ideas given. You can easily tailor the five lessons in each book to meet the specific needs of your group.

▶ *Edge TV* **video series** (Edge Communications; distributed by Youth Specialties, 800/776-8008). Each video in this series (eighteen as of this writing) is loaded with usable bits for generating discussion in your junior high group—not that *Edge TV* is created specifically for junior high. In fact, some material is probably more appropriate for high schoolers. Yet I've found over and over again that no one matches *Edge TV* when it comes to quality video for youth ministry. There are lots of so-so videos—and even some good clones—but none match this series.

▶ *Get 'Em Talking*, Mike Yaconelli and Scott Koenigsaecker (Youth Specialties, 800/776-8008). It's loaded with good discussion starters.

▶ *Junior Highs Only* **series** (David C. Cook, 800/426-6596). These eight books (each with twelve lessons) have been on the market for a few years, but they're still well-written and usable.

▶ *Serious Fun*, David Veerman (Victor, 800/437-4337). Originally two books, they were combined and re-released recently, much to my excitement. This book overflows with creative teaching ideas.

▶ *Talksheets* (Youth Specialties, 800/776-8008). Three titles are specifically for junior high ministry: *Junior High Talksheets*, *More Junior High Talksheets* (both by David Lynn), and *Junior High Talksheets: Psalms and Proverbs* (by Rick Bundschuh and Tom Finley). These reproducible sheets (over 50 in each book) cover an immense range of topics and are extremely easy to use.

▶ *The Handbook of Bible Application* (Tyndale, 800/323-9400). The best thing I've ever found to help me develop outlines for talks. The alphabetical listings are conveniently cross-referenced and lay out good points with accompanying verses. There's even a student version.

▶ **Videos by Curt Cloninger** (Gospel Films, 800/253-0413). *God Views* and *Witnesses* are two of the best discussion starters I've ever seen. The first helps kids wrestle with their misconceptions about God; *Witnesses* helps kids take a closer look at who Jesus was and is.

▶ *Wild Truth Journal for Junior Highers* and *Wild Truth Bible Lessons*, Mark Oestreicher (Youth Specialties/10TO20 Press, 800/776-8008). Okay, so it's a bit gratuitous to include my own titles. But I really believe in these two products. *Wild Truth Journal* contains 50 lessons to get junior highers into the Word of God on their own. And *Wild Truth Bible Lessons* develops 12 of the *Journal's* 50 characters into creative lessons for use in your junior high group.

Continued from page 43

ing topic for weeks to come—unless their mom throws it away.

A huge nail was the best take-home item I ever used. I handed it out the day we talked about Christ's crucifixion. I asked the kids to hold the nail to their wrists and imagine what it would be like to have nails even bigger than these pounded through their wrists. Then I described the details of Jesus' death. Years later I saw those nails sitting on kids' dressers and shelves when I'd visit their homes.

Another prized take-home item is a sucker. Hand them out after your talk about Demas, one of Paul's disciples, who was a sucker for the world (2 Timothy 4:10). Or use the item during class and then send it home. Once we handed out some furry little animals that made this silly honking noise when you turned them upside-down. We had all the kids pet their animals. From there we launched into a talk from our sexuality series on petting and setting guidelines.

Use your imagination. But please, no dinosaur stickers.

GET OFF MY CASE

Case studies are, in the jargon of my current junior high group, "the bomb."

My relationship with God is very strong. He sends angels in my dreams and has been there for me. He's always there.
—*Alexis, 14*

Translation: case studies are highly useful and enjoyable to young teens.

By case studies, I mean hypothetical (or true) situations (three or four sentences is usually long enough) that end in a genuine ethical or spiritual dilemma. Then you ask the question, "What would you do in this situation?" or, "What advice would you give this person?"

Such case studies help young teens shift from concrete consideration of a subject to abstract thinking about that subject (see **Cognitive Development** on page 25). They ease students into applying the lessons you're trying to teach—plus, they get to respond in third person, which is more comfortable for them than first person.

Although intriguing case studies are already written in books like *Tension Getters* (Youth Specialties), you can probably write your own.

MESS WITH IT

No printed curriculum is perfect, as is, for your group. Even the best curriculum must be modified to fit a group's size, locale, demographics, and so on.

All the youth workers at my church are cool, except for one—he always sits by me and talks during the sermon.
—*Steffanie, 13*

So mess with it!

▶ Leave out particulars that won't resonate with your kids.
▶ Ruthlessly scrap teaching ideas you perceive as either too young and patronizing or too mature and abstract for your kids.
▶ Change small or large elements of games.
▶ Rearrange lesson outlines.
▶ Choose a different application.
▶ Use the core of a lesson, but write your own case study.
▶ Use the opening game, but lead into a different Scripture.
▶ Do what you need to better fit the specific needs of the kids you know.

My best lessons come from a variety of sources. One topical study book may give me a good starting point. A book of games gives me an idea that, with a few modifications, leads us further into the subject. Finally I'll add my own ideas to the hopper. After mixing and matching these ideas, I write them into a distinct and purposeful lesson plan that fits my unique group.

My dad's been having an affair, and he doesn't love my mom. But my mom rocks.
—*Charissa, 13*

School is like the 'Power Rangers' TV show—it's boring and pointless.
—*Armand, 13*

FAITH OUTSIDE THE YOUTH ROOM

ON BENDED ROLLERBLADING KNEE PAD

Helping kids develop a prayer life is a huge deal—huge in importance and huge in difficulty. If you want to nurture young teens to become "self-feeding" disciples of Christ, you can't skip over teaching about prayer. But it's tough, especially for kids who grew up on an exclusive diet of ten-minute pastoral prayers on Sunday mornings.

Yet take hope. You can assure young teens of three realities:

1. You can pray anywhere.
2. You can use whatever words you want. No fancy language necessary.
3. God just wants to speak with you.

Jumpstart student prayers by asking them to finish your sentences: "Thank you, God, for—." Invite kids to pray by reading a selected Psalm. Introduce them to the discipline of silence. Set aside time at meetings for them to write out prayers. By using a variety of prayer methods, you teach your kids that there's no one right way to pray.

My school is like a pack of wolves, in that we have one leader and everybody follows her. No one is an individual anymore.
—*Lisa, 13*

49

Marine Boy

Thanks to Desert Storm, our bike trip from L.A. to San Diego experienced a frantic delay.

Approaching Camp Pendleton, a huge Marine base on the Southern California coastline, a small seventh grader drifted behind his group of cyclists and took a wrong turn. At the next checkpoint we realized Steve was missing and went back to look for him. He was nowhere to be found.

We finally returned to Camp Pendleton to request permission to ride through the base to search for Steve. The guards crisply informed us that no groups were allowed inside. The base was on full alert—the U.S., they told us, was invading Iraq.

Sure enough, Steve's wrong turn had indeed taken him into Camp Pendleton. Corralled by a flustered sergeant asking where his adult leaders were, Steve lost what composure he may have had. "I don't know!" he said, and burst into tears.

With a military invasion on his mind, the sergeant didn't have time for a lost junior high cyclist. He passed off the problem by assigning Steve to a team of Marines who were loading cargo onto C-141s headed for the Middle East.

Steve worked all day with the Marines while we drove the California coastline looking for him.

—*Curt Gibson*

GET YOUR HANDS DIRTY

It's easy for typically self-centered junior highers to think of no one other than themselves from dawn till dusk—and then dream about themselves at night. Ironically, these most self-centered individuals find huge satisfaction in helping other people. They just need a little nudge.

So program for service. Give kids a platform for using their hands to help.

▶ Find three elderly people in your neighborhood (not just from your church) who need their lawns raked.

▶ Have your kids sharpen all the pencils in your church pew racks.

▶ Give a fresh finish to a community center or the front porch of a halfway house using donated paint.

▶ Enlist your kids as junior helpers in your church's children's ministry.

TURN OR BURN

Christ is pretty clear on this point: that his followers are to be his ambassadors to the world—including the junior high world. Yet evangelistic outreach among young teens easily degenerates into mere spiritual manipulation. I know this because I've manipulated kids this way.

When you explain the gospel for evangelistic or outreach purposes, consider these common sense pointers:

▶ **Remember that it's God's job to change lives, not yours.** Take the pressure off yourself and your audience. Relax. Share the Good News of Jesus Christ. Offer kids an appropriate way to respond and don't sweat the results.

▶ **Be age-appropriate.** Junior high students greet with blank stares studies on the substitutionary atonement and its connection to man's evil. Distill the truth of the gospel into concepts young teens can grasp. At a recent outreach event, I used the bridge illustration (popularized decades ago by Campus Crusade for Christ's "Four Spiritual Laws"—remember those?) with a stuffed Barney dinosaur as the person (or creature) trying to get to God.

▶ **Use story.** Personal illustrations, contemporary parables, paraphrased Bible stories—stick with narratives and kids will stick with you.

▶ **Follow up.** A clear sign of manipulative evangelism is conversion with no follow-up. If you have students who decide to walk with Christ, fulfill the whole Great Commission (not just the evangelism part) by *making disciples.*

Make evangelistic events attractive to unchurched and non-Christian kids. Communicate to your students that the

There is no such thing as a solo act in junior high ministry; a variety of adults is needed to ensure quality and quantity. Although none of us possess all the qualities that constitute the ultimate leadership model, each of us has qualities to contribute.
—*David Shaheen,* Growing a Junior High Ministry *(Group)*

School will be fun my eighth grade year because I'll be able to help people younger than me without older kids spitting on me.
—*Jennifer, 13*

purpose of the event is for them to invite their friends. Spare no expense. Make the event awesome. Promise your students it won't be a geeky event they'll have to apologize to their friends for. Then keep your promise.

I like church. It's the concept of getting out of bed before church I don't like.
—*Jared, 13*

So You're in Charge?

● ●

Different Kids, Different Programs

Junior highers are all over the map on development, involvement, maturity, and spiritual interest. You simply can't create a one-size-fits-all ministry. Yearly planning for quality junior high ministry must include separate sets of activities that target the following three kinds of kids:

▶ Unchurched, pre-Christian, or disinterested young teens

▶ Regularly attending kids who are at least mildly interested in spiritual growth

▶ The few who really want to be challenged in their faith and held accountable to growth

Take a look at the programs and events you already have going, and choose for each one a clear purpose with features that meet needs of a specific kind of kid. Communicate the purpose for that event to everyone—students, parents, church leaders, other junior high workers. Students need programs targeted right at them— whether they're indifferent to spiritual growth or they're ready to turn the world upside-down for God.

I've accepted God as my Savior and believe in him, although I have a very hard time showing it in my life.
—*Kristin, 12*

THE NO WAY! PRINCIPLE

Every now and then it's worth it to put in the time, effort, and money to really blow your kids' minds. One youth pastor I know overcharged students for every event all year long so he could take his graduating students on a year-end surprise trip to mind-blowing destinations: a cruise one year, the Bahamas the next.

Strong early adolescent ministry creates memories. Some of these need to be the kind that inspire kids to say, "I can't believe we did that! I could never do this anywhere else!"

That's the NO WAY! principle.

Create a NO WAY! sense of awe and excitement on different scales. Make your students gasp "Wow!" by throwing handfuls of candy at them. Or create an event—games and all—around raw fish or Cornish hens (while still frozen, the latter work great for bowling down a tiled church hallway). Sponsor a swim party where everyone enters the pool fully dressed. Cover the floor of your room with a foot of shredded foam rubber. (Look under the FOAM RUBBER heading in your local Yellow Pages for foam rubber scraps.)

NO WAY! activities can be specialized—like chartering a helicopter to take a couple of randomly chosen kids for a ride. (A friend of mine did just this at his camp!)

But it can be just as mind-blowing to kids for you to stop in the middle of a lesson and ask them to turn their handouts into paper airplanes.

You'll find lots of NO WAY! ideas in *Memory Makers* by Doug Fields and Duffy Robbins (Youth Specialties).

BREAK OUT YOUR PITH HELMET

A dozen years ago, when I first started in junior high ministry, I met regularly with a network of seasoned youth workers who specialized in high school work. I was the oddball, for this reason: no one I knew in those days was taking young teens on mission trips, but I wanted to try it.

"Missions should be saved for high school ministry," they all told me. I believed them—for a month or two. Then I stepped out in faith (that's the phrase youth workers use to rationalize half-cocked, risky moves). My first junior high mission trip took us to a Native American reservation in northern Minnesota—a wonderful experience.

After leading 450 kids on dozens of cross-cultural vacation Bible schools and a hundred small construction projects, I'm more convinced than ever that mission trips are good for junior highers. One reason: removed from the clutter of their cultural and physical trappings,

I love going to the big services at my church with my parents—it's really clean.
—*Tara, 12*

55

kids seem more able to hear God. Add to that the fact that they're laying out their lives for God's use, and you have a concoction with more power than Ralph Reed and Ralph Nader combined.

FAMILY FITNESS

Because communication naturally begins to break down between parents and young teens, our work needs to encompass the families of our junior highers. (Make sure your definition of family includes single-parent and blended families.) Work with parents. Communicate information to them until they're sick of you! Provide opportunities for parents to interact positively with their kids.

Two goals direct every family ministry event in our group:

▶ First, we program to create family memories. Kids need to laugh with their parents and play with them. Many families—even good churched families—rarely find time to play together. Creating positive memories enhances a family's daily interaction for months to come.

▶ Second, we work to open clogged lines of communication between parents and teens. Every family ministry event has guided interaction, with parents and teens sharing answers to fun and serious questions. We gently urge kids and their parents to interact. Very little in ministry gives me as much joy as watching family members finish the sentence, "One thing I like about you is—."

BE A (SMALL) GROUPIE

In junior high groups of more than a dozen kids, you must weave small groups into the fabric of your ministry.

If we accept the premise that kids grow in the context of relationships, then by all means we must create a climate that encourages relationships. This relational climate is best birthed with small groups.

Assign students by gender first (mixed gender groups are almost useless). If you need more than two groups, form small groups on the basis of grade. (See **Hundred to One Ain't Good** on page 15 for ratio suggestions.) The changes occurring during the young-teen years make it beneficial to isolate those at different developmental stages for small-group interaction.

Finally, explain to your small-group leaders the New Testament teaching that they are pastors (not that they are ordained in your denomination, but in the sense that they shepherd a small flock of junior highers). Their job descrip-

"I love my parents very much. My dad got a job for two weeks, then got laid off again. He is emotionally sick."
—Mark, 12

tion can be said in one sentence: invest in the kids entrusted to you. (For added punch, read them Matthew 25:14-30—the parable of the rich man who entrusted his money to his servants.)

Think small!

1-900-PARENTLINE

Junior highers are still an integral part of their families. Even if they live in unhealthy situations, their parents still exert more influence on them than their peers (though this changes during their high school years).

This means you'll fight a continual battle if you don't communicate well with the parents of your kids. Avoid these mistakes:

▶ *Mistake 1: Assuming young teens will actually communicate information to their parents.* If you hand out fliers, don't assume they'll get home. If you make announcements, don't assume the information will get to parents or have any similarity to what you actually said. If parents must know certain information, deliver it directly to them—not through their junior high children.

▶ *Mistake 2: Assuming parents are your enemies.* Parents are, or should be, your biggest allies. Keep parents informed

Seven Key Development Needs that Characterize Young Adolescents:
1. Positive social interaction with adults and peers.
2. Structure and clear limits.
3. Physical activity.
4. Creative expression.
5. Competence and achievement.
6. Meaningful participation in families, schools, and communities.
7. Opportunities for self-definition.
—*Peter Scales,* A Portrait of Young Adolescents in the 1990s *(Search Institute)*

and happy, and your group will grow.

▶ *Mistake 3: Assuming your ministry is only for young teens.* Parents can benefit from your insight about their kids. Especially if you're old enough to carry some parenting credibility, parents value your parenting suggestions—books to read, tapes to purchase and listen to, seminars to attend.

▶ *Mistake 4: Assuming parents are incompetent, clueless, or otherwise irrelevant to your ministry.* Young youth workers in particular can get snagged by this absurdity. You may see a few parents who *are* clueless, and then you assume the lot of them are the same. Instead, look to parents for input. Put together a parent advisory team that will support you and give you a parent's perspective.

▶ *Mistake 5: Assuming parents are too old to be good junior high volunteers.* Some of my best volunteers are parents. For the most part, they're dependable and responsible. And they create something young teens have always needed and are getting less and less of these days: a circle of mature adults other than the junior highers' own parents.

Be ready to shock your students with new and creative ideas. After all, they will continually be doing their best to shock you.
—*Steve Dickie and Darrell Pearson,* Creative Programming for Junior High Ministry *(Youth Specialties)*

The Ultimate Tube Run

We'd been to this camp only during the summer, when you could drive from one end of camp to the other on the forest service road. Winter camping, though, was another story. The service road through the camp was impassable in the winter because it cut right through the icy inner-tube run.

Our bus driver was completely unaware of this seasonal feature.

For one day's activities we had asked the kids to meet at the bus early in the morning. By seven o'clock only 10 kids were on the bus, and the driver decided to head over to the other side of the camp to pick up the stragglers.

He drove the closed summer road that cut through the center of camp, arrived at the icy inner-tube run, started to cross it—and lost traction. Slowly but surely the entire bus, 10 kids and all, slid backward down the length of the run.

—*Curt Gibson*

WHO'S YOUR BUDDY?

Let's talk about boundaries. To say "Get a life!" may sound harsh, but it's good advice to well-meaning junior high workers who surround themselves with no one but young teens. Put plainly, junior highers should not be your circle of friends.

Few middle-aged leaders fall into this trap. But if you're in your twenties—especially if you're single—and if you love junior highers, be careful. Passion for ministry to kids easily slips into an unbalanced social circle.

In fact, if junior highers replace your adult friends, you've got a problem on your hands. Either you're allowing young teens' admiration of you to cloud your judgment, or you're a bit overzealous about your calling, or you're in need of therapy. Take a break. Catch your breath. Hang with people your own age. Work at building relationships with peers. It will keep you fresh in ministry.

Caring for your volunteers

Axiom: The spiritual nurture and care that volunteers give to students reflect the spiritual care and nurture volunteers receive from leaders.

If your passion is seeing young teens cared for, then care for the volunteers who serve with you. Volunteers live out what their leaders model for them.

Axiom: Volunteer workers are the best recruiters of other volunteer workers.

Everyone knows it's the paid youth worker's job to say that the junior high ministry is the most exciting ministry in the world. But it carries much more weight when a volunteer says, "I choose this ministry, and I find it fun and fulfilling."

Axiom: Weight whatever budget you have toward development of volunteer staff.

Spending lots of money on games and hoopla is short-term thinking. Well-trained and encouraged leaders (including yourself) are more effective in ministry and less susceptible to burnout.

YOUTH SPECIALTIES TITLES

Professional Resources

Developing Spiritual Growth in Junior High Students

Developing Student Leaders

Equipped to Serve: Volunteer Youth Worker Training Course

Help! I'm a Junior High Youth Worker!

Help! I'm a Sunday School Teacher!

Help! I'm a Volunteer Youth Worker!

How to Expand Your Youth Ministry

How to Recruit and Train Volunteer Youth Workers

How to Speak to Youth...and Keep Them Awake at the Same Time

One Kid at a Time: Reaching Youth through Mentoring

Peer Counseling in Youth Groups

Advanced Peer Counseling in Youth Groups

A Youth Ministry Crash Course

Discussion Starter Resources

Get 'Em Talking

4th-6th Grade TalkSheets

High School TalkSheets

Junior High TalkSheets

High School TalkSheets: Psalms and Proverbs

Junior High TalkSheets: Psalms and Proverbs

More High School TalkSheets

More Junior High TalkSheets

Parent Ministry TalkSheets

What If...? 450 Thought Provoking Questions to Get Teenagers Talking, Laughing, and Thinking

Would You Rather...? 465 Provocative Questions to Get Teenagers Talking

Ideas Library

Combos: 1-4, 5-8, 9-12, 13-16, 17-20, 21-24, 25-28, 29-32, 33-36, 37-40, 41-44, 45-48, 49-52, 53-56

Ideas Index

Youth Ministry Programming

Compassionate Kids: Practical Ways to Involve Your Students in Mission and Service

Creative Bible Lessons in John: Encounters with Jesus

Creative Bible Lessons in Romans: Faith on Fire!

Creative Bible Lessons on the Life of Christ

Creative Junior High Programs from A to Z, Vol. 1 (A-M)

Creative Programming Ideas for Junior High Ministry

Dramatic Pauses

Facing Your Future: Graduating Youth Group with a Faith That Lasts

Great Fundraising Ideas for Youth Groups

More Great Fundraising Ideas for Youth Groups

Great Retreats for Youth Groups

Greatest Skits on Earth

Greatest Skits on Earth, Vol. 2

Hot Illustrations for Youth Talks

More Hot Illustrations for Youth Talks

Kickstarters: 101 Ingenious Intros to Just about Any Bible Lesson

Memory Makers

Hot Talks

Incredible Questionnaires for Youth Ministry

Junior High Game Nights

More Junior High Game Nights

Play It! Great Games for Groups

Play It Again! More Great Games for Groups

Road Trip

Spontaneous Melodramas

Super Sketches for Youth Ministry

Teaching the Bible Creatively

Up Close and Personal: How to Build Community in Your Youth Group

Wild Truth Bible Lessons

Worship Services for Youth Groups

Clip Art

ArtSource Vol. 1—Fantastic Activities

ArtSource Vol. 2—Borders, Symbols, Holidays, and Attention Getters

ArtSource Vol. 3—Sports

ArtSource Vol. 4—Phrases and Verses

ArtSource Vol. 5—Amazing Oddities and Appalling Images

ArtSource Vol. 6—Spiritual Topics

ArtSource Vol. 7—Variety Pack

Videos

Edge TV

The Heart of Youth Ministry: A Morning with Mike Yaconelli

Next Time I Fall in Love Video Curriculum

Promo Spots for Junior High Game Nights

Understanding Your Teenager Video Curriculum

Student Books

Grow For It Journal

Grow For It Journal through the Scriptures

Wild Truth Journal for Junior Highers